Ready to Survive! [2 IN 1]

Ultimate Combo of Survival and Emergency Skills

Bradley Luther

BRADLEY LUTHER

THE ULTIMATE SURVIVAL WAR

Bradley's story begins at the young age of 10 when he becomes passionate about nature, particularly the forests present in North America.

He immediately has an unconditional esteem for the fantastic documentaries of the legendary Bear Grylls and decides to undertake the same type of career.

Thus, equipped with backpacks, flashlights, video camera, and courage, he begins to explore some of the most fantastic forests until the disaster happened ...

Over 72 hours stuck in a cave, with no food and little water left.

For him and his team, it could really be the end but fortunately they were rescued by local rescuers who were passing through…

This terrible experience provides the motivation for Bradley to start all over again with a series of complete survival guides of any kind.

So, if you've decided to venture into the forest this weekend, you might want to read at least one of his guides to make sure everything goes smoothly!

Table of Contents

Survival Manual for Alpha Men

Survival Manual for Alpha Men

----

21 Tactics, Hacks and Techniques to Survive Anywhere and in the Worst

Bradley Luther

Table of Contents

Introduction:

This is the kind of survival book that will tell you how to survive anywhere in the world. Survival manuals have always been a big help for people who think they can do anything no matter what happens. With these tips, you can definitely survive anywhere in the world. Survival manuals have always been known to be good aids in times of emergencies and other unexpected things in life or doing adventures. In this book however, you will be provided with the best ways to survive in any kind of emergency situation.

When it comes to the techniques to survive anyplace in the world, there are several things that you have to know about. One of these is about food and water. You must have water available all the time. You must never run out of provisions. Another technique to survive anywhere in the world is about clothing. You must always dress comfortable as possible.

When it comes to survival guide, the techniques to survive anywhere in the world also include the shelter you need to live. You must learn about emergency shelters that will give you ample protection from the harsh weather conditions and from bugs and other insects. If you do not learn about these shelters when you are a survivalist, you will surely be sorry.

These are the best techniques to survive anyplace in the world but what if there was no survival guide? What would happen then? You will surely starve to death right? Definitely. So what do you need? The techniques to survive anyplace in the world are provided to you in this survival guide.

You do not need to have any special skills for you to survive. All you need is your confidence and boldness to face any hardships that come along the way. A lot of people lacked the confidence and the courage to face their hardships. They are just like timid mice running around in the dark. But you can change that now. Get your survival guide now and start taking life one step at a time.

This survival guide provides you with the best techniques to survive anyplace in the world. Survival does not need to mean dying. It simply means surviving whatever comes your way. This guide will provide you with the courage, confidence, and the skill you need to survive. Learn more about it today. Read more about it online or buy the book.

Chapter 1: Importance and 10 Survival Tips

1.1 Why it is important to learn how to survive in Wilderness

Wilderness survival can be one of the most challenging adventures of anyone's lifetime. Being in the wild and with nature can be an extreme experience.

There is a wide range of arguments answering the question 'Why is Wilderness important?', available on different websites! Arguments come from a very pragmatic sources but also using many emotional arguments, for example :

1.Wilderness Provides Biological Diversity For Both Animal & Human Survival:

Many dangerous animals, plants and microorganisms only find important living and retreat areas in Wilderness. Cross-linked biotopes also increase survival chances for migratory classification.

2. Wilderness for climate protection is critically important:

Healthy forests, moors and flood-plains have a moderate effect on the extreme weather patterns of climate change. It permanently reduces carbon dioxide (CO_2) from air. They give creatures space and time to maintain new climatic conditions to ensure the survival rate of living organisms.

Let's discuss top 21 survival skills and other things you might want to know if ever you find yourself stranded in the great outdoors. These are some common-sense factoids and pieces of life advice that we feel you should consider before you go off on an adventure

Number 1: How to attract attention with a signal or a signal fire

Learning how to attract attention with a signal or a signal fire can be very useful in many different ways. One way is to use it as a signal to draw someone's attention to your vehicle. This can help get your car or truck parked faster, and it can also help you get into a parking space more quickly. Moreover, if you have your signal fixed to warn you of a fire in the area, you can use it to draw attention to a hotspot. The flames from a fire can be quite bright, especially if they are burning close to your vehicle.

Many people who are rushing to get away from a fire may want to use their signal fire to signal to others that they are far away, but they may forget to do so while running towards the fire. In this case, using your signal fire can help others see your location so you can move closer to safety. It may also be necessary for you to run towards the fire if it has spread so that you can get closer to your car before it catches on fire.

Attracting attention with a signal fire is also useful when trying to stop a person from getting out of an area. If you want to stop someone from getting out of a busy area, you can do this by pointing your signal fire at them. Some vehicles may also have "spitter" detectors that can also distract an individual who may be trying to get out of the car. These devices can be used in a similar way to fire extinguishers in that they can distract and warn someone of danger in a place where safety should be the first priority.

As a general rule, knowing how to attract attention with a signal fire should be done before you are ever involved in a fire. If you are in the middle of running towards your car when a fire suddenly breaks out, you can be distracted by the sight of flames and may not see what is really happening. This means that you may not be able to get out of the way in time and may end up hitting the fire. If you are approaching or leaving a building, when you are entering a building, you will want to look around and make sure there are no hazards in the area that could cause you to trip or fall. You should also make sure there are no people lurking in the shadows of the building. Remember that even if you are using a signal fire, some buildings may not allow you to light the structure with a fire extinguisher. In this case, you may need to use another method to scare away intruders or other dangerous individuals. As long as you follow all of the laws surrounding the area, you should be able to safely get into and leave a building.

If you are stuck in a wild area or a forest, then the dead trees in the wild area can be used as a signal fire as they will burn very well. Want to get rescued fast of course, you do first things first.

Gather any combustibles you can find like tinder, kindling and firewood and set up on a hilltop or in a clearing to get maximum visibility. If you don't happen to have matches or a lighter on you, create a spark using a mirror or a magnifying glass and the Sun.

In a pinch your car battery could work too. If you have none of those handy you can always go the old-fashioned route and bang two rocks together or rub two sticks together.

When you hear a helicopter or plane start piling on the branches, the dryer, the better. This will make the smoke thicker and more visible. Do your best to keep the fire going until rescue comes.

You need to make sure that you always use your signal whenever you are in a potentially dangerous situation.

Make sure that you always have the time and place to practice these methods. If you do not practice your flaring techniques, you will never know when an opportunity will present itself so you will have to react prematurely which may end up creating a dangerous situation for everyone involved.

Number 2: How to keep up your dental hygiene

You're stuck in the wild but that doesn't automatically make you an animal. You would want to keep those pearly whites as pearly white as possible and avoid infections or diseases.

So, here's a simple rundown on how to brush your teeth using only things found in the forest as your toiletries.

Find the twig of a non-poisonous and fibrous tree and use that to scrape the gross stuff off your teeth. Obviously, you won't be able to find toothpaste in the wild so you can boil the bark of any tree with tannic acid which includes oaks, birch, hickory, aspen or poplar and use it as a substitute for mouthwash.

It doesn't taste good but you shouldn't care about that. You can find some SAP and chew on that to get all the gunk out of your mouth. If all else fails, just find a stick and chew on it which will clean your teeth as you chew. Just roll it around and chomp on it to get those fibers loosened up.

Number 3: How to tie a bowline

If it's your first adventure, chances are you've never tied a knot other than your shoelaces. It's okay we can work with that all you really need to know to survive in the wild is how to tie a bowline which is an old but easy to tie method of securing rope that can lift a huge amount of weight.

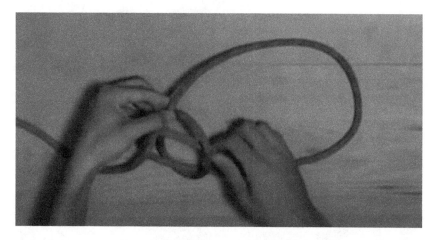

Real outdoor type people use a mnemonic device about a rabbit coming out of his hole running around a tree and jumping back into his hole to remember how to tie a bowline knot and the rabbit comes up out of his hole goes around the tree and gets scared and goes back down his hole and there you go.

What does that mean? In essence you've got to make a loop near one end of the rope pass the other end of the rope up through that loop. Move that end behind and around the upper part of the firstend and then pass it back down through the loop.

Number 4: How to find your way by day or by night without a compass

In the old days, people would use a needle and a map to find their way in the wilderness. They knew (or had learned) how to use these tools to find their way in a foreign land, but now we do not have to use these tools just to find our way in an unfamiliar place. We can find our way just by reading a map or a compass (some still do that), if we know where to look. But for some of us, knowing how to find a way without a compass or a map may seem like more fun. After all, wouldn't it be easier to find your way when you don't need those tools anymore?

Of course, we do not have to rely on a compass anymore just to find our way in the wilderness. We can use Google Earth, the free satellite map program, to help us find our way. There are interactive maps available online, that let you explore the world without relying on your compass.

You need to get off the grid, though. If you live in a modern city, you won't find yourself in the wilderness any time soon. Even if you do get off the grid, though, you will still need a GPS unit to get where you're going. You need to make sure that you have a way to navigate back to civilization.

Fortunately, there are some things that you can do to find your way without a compass or a map. First of all, make sure that you can see your way clearly at night. This is especially important if you are traveling through some dense forest. If you are traveling through the woods at night, you need to be able to see your path very well in order to avoid getting lost. Your map, your flashlight, and your hearing should help you a good deal.

Make sure that you know your way back to civilization, too. If you get lost, you'll have to find a way back to where you started from. Make sure that you have a contact high above on the mountain that you'll be climbing to make sure that you have a way back to the base camp.

Of course, the most important piece of information on how to find your way by day or by night without a map is this: 'Have a good route planned out before you go'. This means that you have to decide where you want to go, when you want to get there, and how you'll get there. If you plan properly, you can go in an organized and smooth fashion.

Now, let's suppose that you have no preparations, so we have to use those old traditional methods in that case. If it's daytime and you have an analogue watch handy you can use that as a compass. Hold it horizontally, if you're in the northern hemisphere, point the hour hand at the sun. If you're in the southern hemisphere point twelve o'clock at the sun.

Bisect the angle or draw a line midway between the hour hand and 12:00 o'clock and you'll find the north/south line, depending on where you're located.

If you don't have a watch look straight up into the vicinity of the sun. It rises from the east and sets towards the west wherever you are. So, you can use that as a good starting point.

What about night time?

Just find the Little Dipper, now find the Big Dipper. Then imagine a line between the two stars at the furthest part of the Big Dipper and connect that line with the handle of the Little Dipper.

This is where you'll find the brightest star which is Polaris or the North Star and it represents the true north.

Number 5: How to perform DIY first aid

When you think of DIY, the images that come to mind are usually construction workers using long tweezers to mend light fixtures or drills in the hope that they'll nail a new door into the wall.

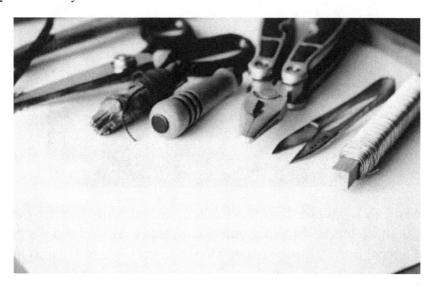

While any amount of effort can be applied to the DIY process, those who want to learn how to do it properly should practice the basics first. Improperly applied DIY first aid skills can result in serious injury if they're not fixed right away. There are numerous ways to ensure that any attempt at DIY first aid is as safe as possible.

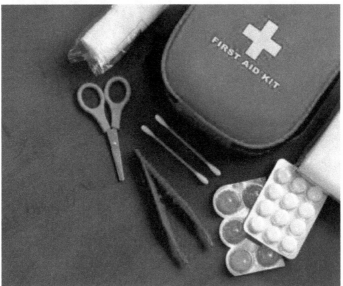

It's important to be aware that the skills involved with DIY first aid aren't the same as those learned from medical courses or from the skills and crafts section of a local home improvement store. If you were to try and learn how to use CPR, for instance, you'd need to train for a year before you could even attempt it on your own. That's because CPR is an extremely specialized skill that only trained professionals should ever attempt to apply. Similarly, while there are plenty of books on CPR that you can buy, it's also smart to make sure that you've had some time to learn how to use the techniques safely.

The best way to get started learning how to perform DIY first aid is to either read about it or talk to someone who's done it before. If you're reading up on it, ask questions at your local library or bookstore, and look online for instructional videos. If you can't find any instructions in print, look online for videos showing you the basics.

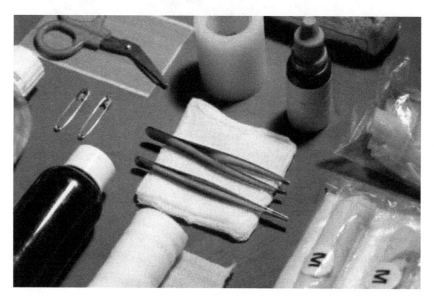

Cardiopulmonary Resuscitation (CPR) as a first Aid:

Once you've learned the basics, it's time to move on to the more advanced methods. One important thing to remember when you learn how to perform CPR is that you should never leave an injured person to die. Even if you think you've done a good job at keeping them conscious, if they stop breathing you have no business keeping them that way. As far as how to do CPR yourself, start by holding the person's hand and moving it towards their chest.

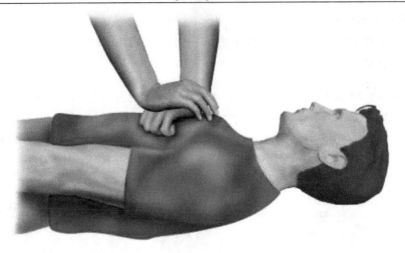

Position Hands Over Sternum

You should then take your other hand (one not holding the person's hand) and slowly move it towards the body and under the chin. Use both hands to grasp the collar and slowly pull the skin down and away from the mouth area. You should also remember to hold your breath and to relax your whole body. It's best to use one hand, preferably the left, to help support the other. Hold the person's pulse points with your fingers and then use the thumb and the index finger of your other hand to gently guide the first aid needle through the blood.

When you know how to perform DIY first aid, you'll be able to use the knowledge to help keep yourself or your friend alive until the paramedics can arrive.

First Aid in wilderness

Have you ever been out in the woods and slipped with your knife or cut yourself with your hatchet and you thought "oh crumb, I forgot my first-aid kit, what am I gonna do now?" So, you're still lost in the wilderness and a bear ate your first aid kit. What do you do? First thing, if you're injured presumably that bear that stole your kit also roughed you up a bit.

You need to clean the wound. Water will do fine for that, but preferably purified water should be your go-to. Obviously we have the ability with a water bottle to cleanse a wound. Next, you'll need some kind of bandage, use a piece of clean cloth or material to cover the wound and apply pressure cooling it down.

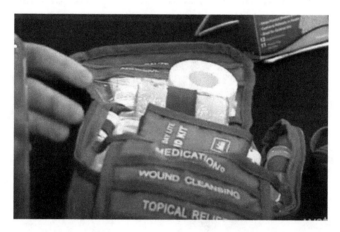

You can cool it down with mud, you can cool it down with sphagnum moss which grows all around in the wild. So, you can pack it with moss, you can wrap it with a t-shirt that gives you compression. If you have duct tape to hold the bandage on, that's even better. Now you'll need to find some old man's beard don't worry, it's a type of lichen, it's green and it grows on tree branches.

You can apply that to your wound as an antibiotic and you should be good to go depending on how serious the wound is.

For those who need more instruction, contact your local emergency medical service. Do yourself a favor and learn how to perform first aid before you try to save somebody else's life.

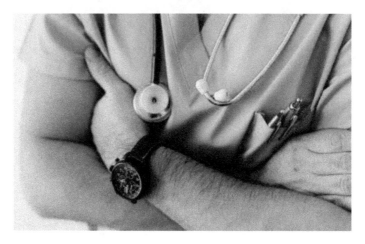

You could learn to do it in a hurry if you weren't afraid of heights!

Number 6: How to Get Water From Plants in Jungle Environments

If you've ever been to the Amazon, South America or other places where people live by the water, you'll know how important it is to get water from plants.

Getting water from plants in jungle environments is not an easy thing to do. There are a lot of snakes, frogs and insects around. It can be dangerous even for the strongest of jungle warriors, if they don't have the right equipment.

In these types of situations, getting water from plants becomes very important. You will need to use a filtration system or something similar. And you'll also need to take special precautions just to stay safe.

So, let's say that you are in the Amazon, or in another environment like Central Africa. At first you may have to walk a long way to get water, depending on where you're going to try and get water from. The longer you walk, the harder it gets. Plus you may need to carry your equipment and water. Then you'll need to take into account the type of water you're trying to get. Do you need rain water? Do you need a pond water feature? Are you in an area where it rains a lot? Make sure that you have a way to purify the water, so that it will be safe for drinking.

Also when it comes to plants in jungle environments, you will need to think about getting a source of water. Many people will bring buckets, but remember that these are living creatures.

This means that insects and snakes could be getting into them and drinking their water. Also make sure you have a source for wastewater or sewage water.

These are just a few things to consider when it comes to how to get water from plants in jungle environments. If you live in an urban area where there is a large water supply, then you may not have to worry about these problems at all. However, if you live in a remote area that does not have many water sources available to you, then you will have to do what you can to keep them clean.

Number 7: Using Woodcraft to Make Chairs and Table etc.

Using woodcrafts to make Chairs and tables in a forest can be a very rewarding experience for children, teens and adults. If you have ever gone to a theme park then you know that most of the trees that are used to create these tables and chairs are live. Why? Because it is cheaper to use live objects than creating something from scratch and it is easier to do the woodcraft at the park.

Most theme parks use woodcrafts in a jungle themed setting. Most of us are familiar with the jungle animals and jungle themed decorating. This is also a perfect time to learn about the beauty of nature and how we need to care for it. Most of the furniture that you will see in a jungle themed area will be made of wood.

Woodcrafts such as chairs, tables and benches are very common. These items can easily be made using simple hand tools using simple woodcraft patterns. You can also learn how to use the various tools available to create a variety of fun jungle decorations. From picture frames, bird houses to furniture, there are lots of different things you can do with wood crafting in Wilderness.

The best way to learn how to make something is by doing it. Bring your own tools with you, or borrow them from a friend. Get some free advice from local people to - people who have been woodcrafting for many years. They will be able to help you make your first project.

The best material to use for this style of crafting is a soft wood such as pine or birch. You can even use cedar and Aspen. But you don't have to stick to pine or birch. As long as it's strong enough, you can use almost any wood you want.

The more detailed the plans, the easier woodcrafting in Wilderness will be. That means you should get some practice. Try making different styles of furniture. Or make a couple of different picture frames. Once you've mastered one design, move onto the next.

A good design always starts with a sketch. Draw the whole thing on graph paper first. Then bring that sketch to life on the piece of wood you're about to make. It's important to make sure your woodcrafting in Wilderness is as detailed as possible. It needs to be a true reflection of what you've imagined. Otherwise, you'll end up making a shoddy job of the wrong design.

When you're about to make something, think of the ways you can improve upon it. Use lighter or darker wood for different parts of a piece. Don't forget to make a rough sketch of your finished product. Then you can go back over it and change anything you think needs to be changed. You can also use woodcrafting in Wilderness to make crafts that other people will enjoy. Go online to find a group of people who enjoy woodcrafting. You can trade tips, ideas, designs and anything else you think can improve someone else's work. You can even make a few extra bucks by selling your pieces. It's possible to make some really good money with wood crafting in Wilderness. You don't need to be super-smarty or knowledgeable. You just need to have a little bit of patience and creativity. You can easily learn how to make crafts by taking classes or buying books on woodcrafting in Wilderness. Soon you'll be creating great products that others will admire.

It is important to remember that you should always learn about safety precautions when working with woodcrafts as these could prove to be very dangerous.

Number 8: Foraging Crayfish

One of the things that makes for a great day in the wilderness is fishing for Crayfish.

Unfortunately, if you are new to Crayfish Foraging then it can be quite a challenge, so before you start out foraging it would be a good idea to get to know your surroundings, know your fish and learn how to forage effectively, which is where a few tips come in.

The biggest tip that you can use when foraging Crayfish in the wild is to know where they are likely to be located.

When foraging crayfish for the first time, it is important to keep a close eye on weather conditions. Foraging in this way during the summer months when it is hot, can be very rewarding, because you might catch quite a bit. However, if it is extremely cold, and raining you could be wasting valuable time.

Foraging Crayfish in the winter is also a great way to catch crayfish because you will have an easier time seeing them. If the foraging activity has stopped all together and you still have some opportunity to fish you should do so, but it is not essential to forage every minute and every second. For those who are new to Crayfish Foraging and are unfamiliar with their environment can sometimes find it difficult to determine where crayfish have been hiding.

If you have no man-made materials you can make traps from natural materials such as honeysuckle. Here is an example of one of these traps made by my friend from bush tools.

What if you have no man-made equipment or tools and you need to catch food fast, for this you can actually use nothing but your bare hands.

Crayfish like to live under rocks and boulders. If the clarity of the water is good, you can often spot them crawling around on the riverbed.

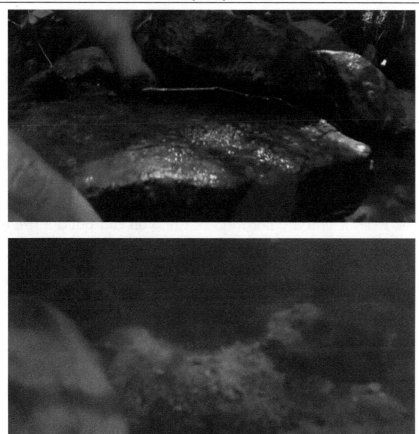

If you are quick you can pin them to the ground avoiding their pincers. They taste incredible and you can either boil them or cook them directly over a fire.

You should also try to use as many types of bait as possible while foraging for crayfish. Crayfish will generally eat any type of food, so try utilizing either live or frozen foods that they are accustomed to. If you are new to Foraging Crayfish, or even if you have been foraging crayfish for quite a long time, it may be a good idea to use jigs as well. Try using them as lures during some of your foraging trips.

Number 9: How to Build a Fire in Wildfire

One of the most fun activities is learning how to build a fire in the wilderness. Even if you are not fond of fire, you can build a fire easily as long as you follow some important tips. Here are some tips on how to build a fire in the wilderness. This will also help you make your own fire as well. Just follow these simple steps and you will be off to a great start.

Place stone around the place you have planned to build a fire. If there are some marshy lands nearby, then dig some holes in those for the stone to rest in. Make sure you cover all the places with sand to avoid the smell of wet wood. Step inside the holes and put the stone inside.

Step One: Using a small flat piece of wood, place a log inside the small hole and cover it with dirt. The dirt should be loose so that the log does not shrink or stick inside the small hole. Draw some lines around the log to show where the hole should be. Use a pencil to draw the lines clearly.

Step Two: Using larger sticks, place these around the log. Make sure you secure the sticks firmly with dirt. Once the soil is secure, use the flat piece of wood to support the logs. Windbreak the large sticks in around the log.

Step Three: Spread some tinder on the ground near the fire. When tinder becomes wet, it can start to ignite. If tinder still does not catch fire, cover the hole with dry twigs or dry branches. Use some clean dry cloth to wipe the surface of the rocks and the ground. Place your now ready-made firewood in the hole and light the tinder.

Step Four: Use some larger sticks to place around the fire as well as dry pine needles. Place them tightly against the rocks. Allow them to remain there for about thirty minutes. Once they are all burned, produce enough heat to start a small piece of coal. Light the coal and use this to start the process over again with the other pieces of wood.

Step Five: Build a fire in the wilderness that uses dry materials. Place some clean dry logs in the bottom of the fireplace and then build up more logs at the top. You will need enough wood for everyone involved. After you have built enough pieces for everyone, sprinkle some charcoal over them. Allow the charcoal to smolder for about twenty minutes before placing the fire back into the fireplace. When you do this process, you will begin to produce sparks from the fire.

Step Six: If the wood has not produced any sparks, you may want to try using an electric bow to create them. If you are not comfortable firing the bow, then you can simply use a small piece of wood as well as some dried twigs or pieces of paper to create the fire. Place the wood at the top and then bring it down slowly over the open piece of paper. You can use the bow to help generate more and stronger sparks. Continue in this manner until you produce plenty of free hot coals.

Number 10: How to Gather moss in Forest - Use Nature's Resources

The best time of the year for collecting moss is in summer or fall when trees are producing their fruit and new growth is occurring.

The type of tree you get will affect how to gather moss in the forest, but there are several common types. Each has its own way of production that must be taken into consideration.

One of the most common types of moss is deciduous trees such as oak, birch and maple. This type of mosses is usually small and dark green in color and can grow on a tree without being noticed. It forms bundles or mats under the tree where it matures and releases itself in the air.

The easiest way to learn how to gather moss in the forest is to follow nature. Observe what trees in the area are producing and how many branches they have. The thicker the tree the more moss will grow and there are two types. One is needlelike and the other is scalloped.

Needlelike mosses grow in clusters and look like large mushrooms. They are usually very fine and powdery and can hide in the smallest spaces. Scalloped mosses are the thickest and can be spotted easily. The branches of this type of moss can reach very high and trees can collapse if the branches are weak or break off. There are many ways to determine whether a tree is needlelike or scalloped and you can do so by taking a branch and examining it closely.

If you are learning how to gather moss in forest one important aspect is moisture. You need to look for moisture either on the moss itself or in the soil beneath it. Moisture will help the moss grow and spread out but if it is not kept up the moss will not spread. Moss in wet areas will start to shrink and if it is too much it will even die.

Collect as much moss as you can, it is worth preserving. If you find a good spot to collect then use it repeatedly to create new molds that will improve the quality of your moss. You can save the tree bark and the moss together and make a really unusual decorative mixture that will last a long time.

If you are looking to put the moss into a pot, then be sure that you will be able to dry it out before you place it into the pot. The first few times you try to mold moss, you may find that it keeps growing until you pour water on it, then you realize that the tree bark has died and the moss is ready to be used.

Chapter 2: Top 11 Survival Tips

Number 11: How to make a spear to catch animals and food

You've got a fish on your spear and are trying to stab it out to get him, to kill him so that you can bring him back but it ends up getting away. Here's a handy tip for catching cute little forest creatures or small marine animals for consumption.

A split tip gig is a multi pronged spear that quickly snatches critters from the forest floor or in a body of water. You want me to make a spear? We need you to make wonderful fishing. Find yourself a small sapling about an inch around and cut the thicker end into four parts.

Going about ten inches down from the top out, spread those tips up. Use a stick to spread the parts and then make sure they're good and sharp with a rock or knife. Finally, use that gigtube, we can spear anything from snakes to chipmunks - rats, raccoons, bears, fish etc.

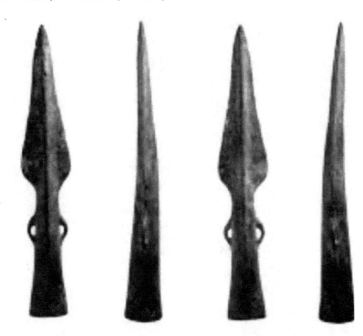

Learning how to make a spear to catch fish and animals in the wild is not as difficult as one may think. In fact, it can be quite easy, provided that you know how to handle your weapon properly. Spearheads can be in many different shapes and sizes, which make them great for hunters who want to use something more than just a stick or a branch to dispatch their prey. A spear is generally made out of metal or wood, but there are some materials out there now that are particularly effective in boating.

The first part is choosing the right type of spear. The most common type is a long stick, but there are also smaller ones available, as well as those that look more like the end of a hook. A spearfishing stick is typically made out of wood or metal and is either fixed in place or lightweight enough to be carried around. This is usually the best choice for those who are just starting out, as it is easy to learn how to use it. If you have experience, however, a fixed spearfishing pole is probably better since you will be able to get some practice using that while practicing your new skills.

Once you have the right type of spear, you need to find where the fish are biting. This is an important part of learning how to make a spear to catch fish and is often done with the aid of a guide. A guide can help you find the best places to spearfish, so that you can stay safe and get the fish you want. If you are spearfishing in wild waters, you can sometimes even get away with not bringing your spearfishing equipment with you. This is because some rivers and streams do not have any restrictions on the type of equipment you can use, so long as it is not considered illegal or dangerous to use them. However, if you are spearfishing in a state park or another body of water that is off limits, make sure you bring your spear with you so you can be assured that it will remain legal.

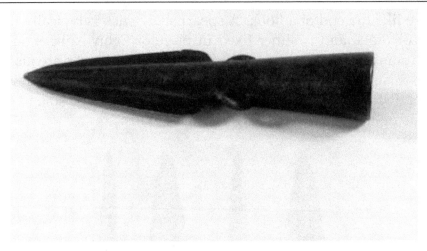

It is also important that you take care of your spear. You do not want it damaged or scratched because it might come into contact with a sharp object, such as a bolt, hook, or other part of the fish's body. Before each use, wash the spear in hot soapy water. You can also wipe it down with a damp cloth to remove any soap residue or dirt that might accumulate on it. Wipe it down carefully, but try not to move it around too much, so that it does not become jagged or damaged.

If you learn how to make a spear to catch fish and practice using the proper techniques, you will find that you will be able to use this skill for many seasons to come. You might be surprised at how quickly you learn how to shoot your spear accurately and with little effort. You might even be able to go out in the wilderness and find fish right away, which is a very exciting feeling! Your friends might surprise you as well, because many people have heard of someone using a spear to catch fish, but never realized that they actually did it themselves.

Spear-fishing is fun, easy, and exciting. You should take the time to learn all of the basics that you can before heading out on your first trip. The wild world out there is waiting to feed on your success. Spearfishing is not a new sport, but it is one that has been growing in popularity lately. Now is the time that you discovered it, so that you can make the most of your time out on the water.

Number 12: How to find food?

When these are compact and green, you can eat those, some people who boil those up and cook them that way. If you don't have a split tip gig, you'll need to get food another way.

Before you become food for something else, your best bet is to find a guide that tells you which berries and flowers are edible. If one isn't handy which it probably isn't, if you're lost in the wilderness then you can use the good old fashioned method of trial and error.

Remember this rhyme 'white and yellow kill a fellow, purple and blue good for you'. But beware, while this approach might allow you to survive longer, it might also kill you immediately. Come on now! it's got to be a little cautious. I mean that book of yours is cool and everything but you can't depend entirely on leaves and berries.

If you'd rather not leave your survival to chance there are a few rules of thumb to adhere to avoid plants with milky or discolored SAP. 3 leaved growth patterns, almond scented leaves, anything like seeds that are inside pods and things that look like mushrooms.

Wild food sources are very important for our health and survival. There are many types of wild foods such as berries, nuts, wild greens, mushrooms, and many more. It is up to us to know how to find food in the wild for daily consumption.

Many people want to have a wonderful vacation and experience nature. But many also want to do something for the environment so that we can all leave our trash in a better place instead of taking it on the trip and leaving it for dead or dying animals to eat.

If you are on a vacation in the wild and need some food for you to stay, you may wonder where you will find it. The answer is not difficult if you use your imagination. There are many sources of food in the wild that you can find while enjoying your vacation. One of these sources are insects.

There are many types of bugs and other insects that can be your food source while you are out there. They are usually easy to find because they are small and easy to miss. You may also be able to find other bugs that you can eat as well. Another food source is plant matter. There are many types of plants and some are edible. You may be able to find fruits and vegetables as your main food source as well.

When looking for a food source in the wild, you need to look around and see what you can forage for. Look for areas where there are insects feeding on the insects that live in your area. If you cannot find a food source in the wild there is another option of finding things that are edible.

You can find a variety of different foods from mushrooms to salami to squirrel repellents. If you can find these types of things you can eat them to get them back into shape for some of the times when you are not camping with your friends or family.

Camping can be a fun time for many people. However, you need to know how to find food in the wild west. It is important to take your food supply with you to camp, so you will have it once you get back from the campground.

The best way to find something edible to eat while you are in the wild west is to keep a food diary. Once you get familiar with the foods you will see the type of things that you will eat. Good luck!

Number 13: How to build a fire?

If you do manage to get some food, you might need a fire to cook it but even without food you need to keep yourself warm. First and foremost, you'll need tinder not the app although, we suppose that's one way to keep yourself warm.

Tinder in this case refers to small stocks that will easily turn a spark into a full-blown fire. The best tinder you could use is a shareable tree bark.

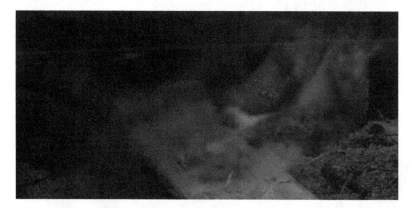

Break those up into even smaller bits, find an area to make your fire and create shelter from the wind by using a log or something big.

Then stack your kindling preferably branches of different sizes in a conical shape. This will facilitate the passage of oxygen to your fire which will make it grow. If you don't have any of the items mentioned in our signal fire entry, then you can use flint to spark the fire or again rub two sticks together.

When it starts to grow then you can begin to add bigger kindling. You could build fire extenders that would be things out of pine pitch or even birch bark or other easily ignitable material. Also don't forget to scavenge the area for any other material.

You can use it to keep yourself warm like leaves, pine branches or the skin of an animal you've hunted for food.

Number 14: How to build a shelter?

Well, It looks like you're gonna be here for a while and may as well get comfortable. You'll need to find a dry area preferably one that's flat elevated and protected from the elements. By a cliff wall look around for a strong tree.

Seeing white oak trees and pale models to build with this is a good spot. Ideally you want your tree to be at an angle but if that's not the case then grab a big branch from the ground, lean it against a strong tree and start stacking smaller branches on one side to make a wall.

Once, this is done, find leaves moss and other forest debris and start covering the wall as well as the ground to keep you warm. When you're finished, get cozy and pray that the wind doesn't pick up. This is what I might call a backwoods timeshare. No honorable mentions this time.

Wild animals have been our friends for a long time and it is our responsibility to look after them in the wild. They will come to harm in our homes but what else can we do.

When I was a kid I used to watch my dad putting up a shelter for the birds. There is nothing more beautiful than watching birds and squirrels in their natural habitat. It is easy to build a shelter on your own but you need to be sure that you have all the building materials that you need.

The shelter does not always need to be outdoors, you can build one in your backyard. If you live in an area that has cold winters then you need to build a shelter that will protect you from the cold winter weather. There are so many different kinds of shelters that you can build and I would suggest that you visit your local stores and see what they have to offer you.

The shelter that you build will depend on the size. A big shelter will probably take a lot of work to build. You will need to build it at least ten feet higher than the ground so that animals cannot get into the shelter.

Smaller shelters need to be built in such a way that they are level. If you build a shelter with uneven ground then animals could easily slip through the cracks. You should also make sure that you secure the foundation of the shelter to prevent water from flooding inside it.

You can build a shelter anywhere in your yard as long as you have enough room. You do not need to put it on top of anything because the ground is usually enough for it to stand on. You can build a wooden shelter or you can use stone. Both of these shelters will give shelter from the wild animals and you do not even have to worry about termites.

If you are a handyman or woman, then I would highly recommend building your own shelter. It is not as hard as you think it is. All you need is the right plans and a little bit of building experience. You can learn how to build a shelter in wild animals by searching the internet or checking out some books at your local library. There are a lot of great places to find information on how to build a shelter in less than an hour. You can be up and building a shelter in no time at all.

Building your own shelter is a great project for the kids to do. It gives them responsibility and teaches them how to be responsible. They can learn a lot by taking care of the wild animals that live in your yard. It will also teach them about nature. If you are someone who likes to spend time outdoors, then building a shelter is a great project for you to take on. I am sure that once you learn how easy it is to build a shelter for your animals, you will never want to go back to the store bought versions again.

Number 15: How to Find Clean Water

If you want to find water you must first find dirt. There's probably nothing more important to your survival than good fresh water.

That you find in a puddle or stream is a safe bet but only if you boil it. We told you that fire would come in handy, if you can't do that then collecting rain snow or Dew is also a great way to get yourself something drinkable.

To get enough of the stuff to keep you alive, you can soak the liquid using a rag or some type of fabrics like a shirt or bandana. Then squeeze the water out. You can also tie a bag around a leafy branch to collect the water from a tree's transpiration which is also drinkable. If you happen to find a cactus, you can slice it open for some refreshing h2o as well. Because there's so much of this that's where getting the fluid through, just a munch and suck finally and perhaps most deliciously. You can also quench your thirst with the syrup from a maple tree, awesome! What it boils down to is that staying safely hydrated is the name of the game with any luck at all in a few hours so long as the sun stays out.

Number 16: How to Light Fire With Flint and Steel

I remember when I was a child, my father always told me that if I wanted to do something dangerous, I should not try to do it on my own. He used to say that there would be too much danger involved in fire. So, I never did anything crazy or experimental until I was older. But, when it comes to learning how to start a campfire and start lighting the fire, many people wonder the same thing.

You can make use of either flint or steel for the fire starting materials. You should call for any help that is available if you don't know anything and make sure that you are safe.

You may be wondering how to start a fire with flint and steel? You should know that it is actually not that difficult if you follow some basic steps. If you follow these steps carefully, then you will surely have a good time during camping trips, barbeques, and other recreational activities.

First of all, you should gather all the flints that you need. You can use paper or cardboard to keep them in one bundle. The bundle should include several pieces of flint such as split pieces of flint, flakes, sand, and small pieces of shavings. Make sure that you have enough pieces of flint so that you will not run out while you are trying to start a fire.

After you have gathered all the flints, you should also make use of some newspaper to soak up the water that is left over after you have started to heat up the fire. It is important that you cover up the newspaper so that the smoke and smoky residue will not fall into the food that you will serve. Once the fire has already started, you should cover your nose and mouth so that you will not breathe in the smoke. You can also use a face mask if you do not feel comfortable breathing in smoke.

After you have covered your nose and mouth with the paper, you should remember to inhale the steam from the steel pan through your teeth. You should take a few deep breaths in order to bring the steam to your mouth and throat. Inhaling the steam will help you relax your body muscles and it will also help to clear the sinuses. You must remember to keep your hands away from the flames. Once you have done these things, you will be able to get the job done right and you will never be confused about whether you should continue or stop.

Number 17: Retaining water in Wild

There are many techniques you can use to locate and collect water. Sometimes a simple understanding of geography might be all that you need to take this shot. For example, you will notice a valley with two steep sides, this v-shaped valley was formed hundreds of thousands of years ago by glaciers carving their way through the softer rock. What it leaves behind is these valleys in the shape of a 'V'. At the base of these valleys there is a very high chance that you will find a river stream or some form of flowing water. But how do you find water in areas where there are no fresh running rivers, streams or lakes? The climate you're in is hot and arid. If you have a plastic bag, you can tie this around some leaves at the tip of branches on small trees and shrubs.

Wait a few hours and the sun will encourage evaporation to take. This water vapor that comes out of the leaves will begin to condense and water droplets will begin to form on the inside of the bag. In this example, it is the beginning of June and the outdoor temperature is 24 degrees Celsius you can see that within 10 minutes of placing this bag on the leaves. It's beginning to show condensation and just a few hours later you can begin to see water droplets forming on the inside of the bag although not much. These might well be the vital few drops of water you need to survive.

If you have no containers to collect water you can either use a tarp or even use any cloth type material. Hang it out in the rain and allow it to absorb water afterwards wringing it out to collect the rainwater it will hold this water for a while so you can carry it with you.

As you move you can also make a wooden cup from a small log just split it into four sections, carve a small notch in the bottom end of these sessions.

Number 18: Creating a Ferrocerium Rod Fire

There are many different ways to light a fire. Fire has helped humans to survive for thousands of years and it is still used to this day in our everyday lives.

The ability to be able to light a fire in the wilderness is one of the most essential skills that you can have in a survival situation. If you have a ferrocerium rod in your kit you can light so many different types of natural materials.

One of the best and most effective pieces of natural material for this is the bar from a silver birch tree.

Simply scrape the outer bark into small shavings. Shower it with sparks from your Ferro rod and it won't be long until you have a flame. This can also be done in wet conditions, when the bark is done.

Number 19: Light fire by Bow drill method

The next method is primitive fire by friction technique. A common friction fire lighting method is the bow drill. Using a thin stick as a spindle at another stick, cut to a flat shape to make a half board. You can begin to make your fire. You will need another stick to make your bow using some cordage.

Wrap this around at both ends of your bow and attach it to your spindle. By twisting it, burning the board first with a few slow and consistent movements. Cut a small notch with your knife. This is for collecting the dust that you will create once your hearth board is ready. Begin to work the bow and spindle back and forth increasing downward pressure.

As you do so, when you start to see smoke don't stop, keep going for a few more seconds. You should have yourself an ember. Allow this Emberto establish and then place it in a tinder bundle and blow it to flame. Getting the ember is not the hard part but getting the ember turning into a flame can be tricky.

There are a few factors that you need to consider such as the type and dryness of the wood that you are using. Plus the climate and conditions that you are in practice in humid conditions, cold conditions and wet conditions.

But what if you have no cordage to make a total, how do you then light a fire? The hand drill is an even more rudimentary form of a bow drill and it is much harder to master.

It still utilizes the same principles through friction heat and oxygen to help you get that flame.

Number 20: Foraging Wild Edibles

It takes time and patience to learn this method, but it is a key survival skill to know having the knowledge of where your food comes from and how it arrives on your dinner plate.

Every day is something that we should all have a good understanding of. The ability to harvest your own food from the wild is key to turning a survival situation into a comfortable thriving environment.

Having a good foundation knowledge of basic wild edibles is a good place to start, as you generally won't need any tools or equipment to gather them.

For example, the humble stinging nettle Ithaca diosa. Despite its appearance and all-too-common stinging properties, it's actually packed full of vitamin A, Vitamin C, iron, potassium, manganese, and calcium.

In its peak season, nettle contains up to 25% protein dry weight which is high for a leafy green vegetable.

The leaves can also be dried and used to make herbal tea. It has been used to treat disorders of the kidney, cardiovascular system, influenza and gastrointestinal tract.

The stem of the plant contains bast fiber which can be used to make cordage. There are many more uses for this plant. However you cannot survive on nettles alone at some point. You will need to up the fat and protein content in your diet. So, that your body doesn't waste away.

Number 21: Drop Net Method

Another form of catching your own food is by net. The net can be incredibly effective when placed in the right area but this is more of a passive fishing technique.

A drop net however can be a great way to catch crustaceans such as crab and lobster.

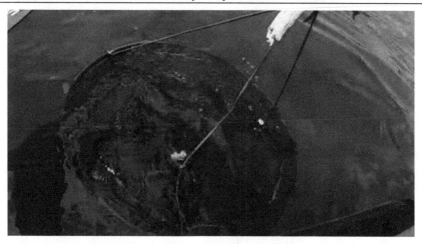

Simply put some bait in the net, making sure it is secure and drop it down to the sea bed. After 30 to 40 minutes, pull the net up to check your bait. If you want to be more active with your foraging, swim down and grab your crustacean directly from the net.

The benefit of this form of fishing and foraging is that you can drop multiple nets across a wide area giving you a greater chance of catching fish.

Conclusion:

When you combine all of these four pillars i.e fire, water, food and shelter together that's when you can begin to thrive which leads on to the fifth and final pillars of survival and that is the ability to thrive. Once you have access to food, fire, water and shelter you can begin to make life more comfortable for yourself. For example you can use bushcraft and woodcraft to create tables, chairs benches, cooking grains, pot hangers and much more. This will help you to keep your mind occupied and it will allow you to focus on thriving in the environment that you're in.

Techniques to survive in the wilderness are easy if you know how to use them. Another technique to build your survival skills in the wilderness is to build shelter. Shelter can be as simple as a plastic tent to a cabin or log house. It should be well-built enough to withstand any weather condition. You can also learn to build your own emergency kit in the wilderness. This is essential especially if you encounter an emergency situation in the middle of wilderness. For example, if you come across a body of water, you should have a raft or a boat in order to safely cross it. In the same way, a bear should also be caged. This can be done by hanging a rope around his neck and a big stick over his eyes.

Thank you for reading this book. If you enjoyed it please share it with your friends.

Effortless Foraging for Survival [with Pictures]

Identify, Harvest and Use the 9+1 Useful Edible Wild Plants of North America

Bradley Luther

Table of Contents

Introduction

If you want to learn how to survive easily in the wild, then you must have to read this book. I will be talking about my observations and opinions about edible plants in the wild, their edible varieties, and their effects on foraging success. This information will help you determine what types of survival equipment is best for your survival. You will also learn what to do in certain situations to make foraging even easier and more successful. After reading it, I am sure that you will have some new ideas on what to bring along on your next trip out into the great outdoors.

When foraging for food in the wild, it can be very helpful to know what edible plants are available to you, and which ones you should avoid. There are many plants out there that can make for excellent meals, but most people don't know where to find them. This book will cover some of the edible plants that are good for foraging and those that should be avoided.

They can also be used as herbal remedy that has been used for centuries as a treatment for colds, flu, and other general ailments. It is a wonderful aid for insect bites, wounds, digestive upsets, and stomach issues. It acts like antibiotics and antiseptics and should be consumed as directed. You can make tea from the leaves, which is good for soothing insect bites. You can store the leaves in a container for later uses, or you can eat the entire plant.

Chapter 1: Basics of Foraging

1.1 Choosing Your Edible Plants

Foraging for survival in the forest can be tough and many foragers make the mistake of relying on the wrong kinds of edible plants for sustenance. You must understand that the foraging strategy is to take what the plant in no way offers you but to also make use of the plant's other beneficial characteristics. Some of these are: tolerance to the cold, tolerance to low light, and photosensitivity. Let us look at how you may utilize these characteristics of a plant for your survival in the wild.

If you have to forage for edibles in a harsh environment then you would want to consider eating the plant straight from the ground. In this way you would also increase the chances of getting hold of plant food that has had time to form its own nutritious internal enzymes and starch reserves.

You may not have the luxury of storing such food for later consumption. Even if you do store edibles like this for later use, the chances that they will survive are quite minimal.

However there are some edible plants that have developed a resin coating on their leaves that can resist the harsh conditions in foraging areas. Even the hardiest of the varieties will decay fairly quickly when foraging after sunset. If you are a forager who values survival of the fittest then the types of edible plants that we will discuss further may be an excellent choice as a food source.

1.2 Foraging Equipment

Another consideration that you have to take into account when foraging for edibles is the survival of your foraging equipment. Foraging equipment may not be very robust. It may simply break down after exposure to the elements for several days or weeks. If you are planning to carry on foraging activities for weeks or months then it makes good sense to invest in durable and robust equipment. Fortunately there are many quality survival equipment items on the market today that are suitable for long term foraging and which can make for an excellent addition to your emergency food supply.

1.3 Health Consciousness

The other consideration you have to take into account when foraging for wild edibles is your health. Wild edibles can be contaminated with a number of harmful insects and viruses. These insects and viruses can present serious health risks if consumed. Some of the insects and viruses that can threaten wild edibles are: Sarcoptes scabei, Q fever, botulism, Trypanosomia, Rhizopus, Echinococcus, Clostridium Botulinum, and Mumps.

There are also a number of parasites and worms that are attracted to plants that are foraged for. Parasites such as: whip-worms, hookworms, lice, and even ticks, are just a few of the health hazards that can pose a threat to people foraging for wild edibles. To be healthy, always clean the plants with fresh water and even boil it if possible.

A final consideration is the time of year for which the foraging activity will take place. For most edible plant species forage will be more easily achieved in the spring months. The plants have a longer developmental time and also have an increased metabolic rate. Edible plants that are more easily maintained in the spring months include wild onions, carrots, spinach, and raspberries. These edibles are particularly useful foragers because they are not subject to significant alteration in their growth pattern.

You are on an adventure in the wilderness, but my god, you've just run out of food. So what will you do? Starve to death? No, not today as here are top of the most common edible wild plants, fruits and trees that you can eat while out in the wilderness.

Chapter 2: Wild Edibles for Foraging

2.1 Primrose

First up, we have the 'Primrose aka Primula vulgaris'. One of the first plants to emerge during the spring but often as early as winter. This herb is one of the most popular herbs around. In fact, it was named after primrose, the first plant that has been cultivated for medicinal purposes. Primrose is very aromatic and grows in groups of three to six plants. It is mostly used as a flavoring for teas and capsules.

For harvesting, leaves of the herb are removed and put in a room where there is no air and it will die within a few weeks without fresh air. It can also be dried and stored. The herb is said to be more effective if it is harvested in autumn. Some people claim that this type of herb gives better health benefits than other traditional herbs.

When harvesting the herb, there are some tips that you must follow. You need to harvest the leaves and the plant stems at the same time. It is best if you do it in the early morning or evening so that the heat does not affect the herb. If you want to be safe, you can cut the plant in a specific direction so that the heat will not go to waste and the herbs will stay healthy.

For harvesting the herb, you can use a knife or any sharp object that you have. Do not be too eager to cut the leaves because they contain a lot of essential oils that you should leave for later on. If you find that the plant is very brittle, then you can use a leaf blower or press the buds. If you are harvesting and using your own herb, then you should read the instructions on how to cook and use the herbs properly. You can even find some tips and recipes on the internet for additional help.

Once you are done harvesting, you need to clean the leaves thoroughly. This should also be done immediately so that they are easy to absorb. In order to preserve the health of the leaves, you can use them as a seasoning. You can make flower bread or salad sandwiches with the leaves.

The woodland dwelling Primrose is an abundant source of food during seasons where that can be scarce. An impressive and bushy plant composed of numerous tongue shaped leaves and pale yellow flowers. But to accurately identify a plant you must scrutinize over its smaller finer details.

Its leaves are broad and are deeply wrinkled and craggy. It has a prominent white midrib running down the length while underneath, it is a much paler shade of green with a light coating of fuzzy hairs and it's pale yellow flowers have five individual notch metals that turn an egg yolk yellow towards the base.

Unlike many other plants, its leaves don't grow out of the flower stems. Instead they are a 'basal rosette' meaning that they all grow out of the ground in a somewhat circular cluster. Once all of those features have been met then you can be certain that it is a Primrose. What a delight that would be as all parts of this plant are edible. The flowers and stalks can be eaten raw as can the craggy and crinkled leaves which have a pleasant and slightly sweet taste very similar to that of lettuce. Although it is a spring bloomer, this plant can also be found throughout the summer and far into autumn so there's certainly no shortage.

You may also find it in orange or violet colored varieties but pale yellow is the most common color. If the leaves and flowers don't quite fill you up then you may be interested in its large and extensive root network.

Stick your knife in the ground and pull up the locks to reveal the noodle-like network of tasty edible roots full of carbs and high in energy. Just take them down to the stream to rinse away any dirt and you've got yourself a ginormous mound of survival food, full of carbs, calories, sugar, starch and fiber.

The bountiful Primrose is a substantial source of life-sustaining nourishment and considering that it is more or less available all year round. That makes it an absolutely essential edible plant to become familiar with. Although everything you see here is edible that does not necessarily mean that it is clean and so if you have the option then you should always boil your foods.

First in a cup of water to clean and partially cook them this is not essential but it is a best practice and that applies to all of the items.

2.2 Thistle

Thistle plant has many health benefits that make it great to consume as a food or supplement. There are some groups which would also like to promote their community's awareness of this plant. To emphasize further the appeal of using this plant in the home or wild for cooking and medicinal purposes, people prefer to make use of different methods in harvesting this plant.

In the spring harvesting of Thistle plant should be done earlier in the season since the leaves and stems are still in good conditions for preservation. Early harvesting promotes the best use of the plant. It is more nutritious and safe to use because there are fewer weeds around it, hence less danger in using it.

A familiar sight along the hedgerows and tree lines the common thistles are easy to spot.

Harvesting of Thistle plant can also be done in the fall. Fall is the best time to gather this because the risk of getting the weeds is not much. In the fall harvesting of Thistle can be done in two ways. The first way is to use a mechanical harvester. It is advisable to not to use this method since it might cause the tearing down of other helpful plants. The second way of harvesting Thistle plants is through hand. It is a better way of harvesting because there is more safety with the use of human hands. Also, using hand to harvest the Thistle leaves and stems reduces the risk in getting the weeds underneath the surface. It is considered as safer than mechanical harvesting.

Due to their bulbous eruption of purple flowers which later turn into those fit clouds of fluffy seed, notorious for its many prickly spikes.

All parts of the plants are covered in unwelcoming spines and prickly brax. With each of those dark green leaves being host to a very sharp stiff needle at the end of each lobe.

A nuisance to handle but fortunately for those looking for food. It is the root of the fissile that is edible. In the spring this is an easier job, put the knife in, lift up and pull out to reveal the thick and substantial lengthy tap roots which are full of carbs, sugars and calories.

A good survival food that contains everything a starving person would need.

You can eat them raw just like a carrot or a stick of celery and the leaves and stalks of the fissile are technically edible too providing that you cut away all of those sharp needles and brax.

2.3 Fireweed

They are impressively tall and showy, when fully grown the fireweed plant will stand up upward to 8 feet tall.

It is often found growing and mass in ginormous colonies in woodland clearings and riverbanks. Noticeable from a distance the purple and green spikes of fireweed will feature smooth slender stems which are host to four petals bright purple flowers.

A series of diagonally climbing seed capsules and their signature dark green lance shaped leaves. Each leaf is slim, narrow and pointed and much like a Primrose, it has a significant white midrib running down the length.

In the autumn those seed capsules split and erupt into seeds resembling thick fluffy plumes of candy floss which makes for a good on-the-fly flash tinder if you're ever in need of fire-making materials.

All parts of the fireweed plant are edible. The narrow leaves, the shoots, the stems and the flowers.

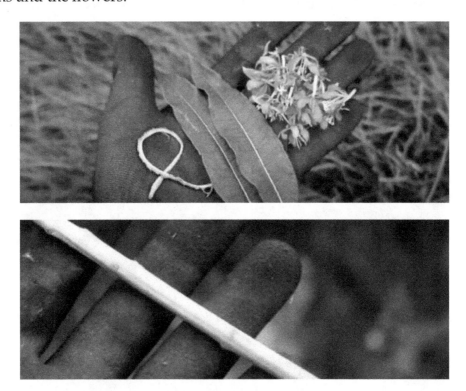

But the real amazing part of fireweed is the pith that's found in the center of the stem. Do split the stem down the middle and use a knife to scrape out the edible pale green pit which is full of nutrients and is quite tasty.

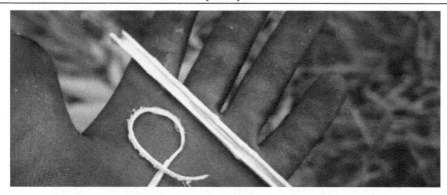

You can eat it raw, no need to clean and you may also be surprised to find that it tastes very similar to cucumber. As an aside in Siberian culture, the fresh leaves of fireweed are brewed into hot water to make a tea known as Kapur. Perhaps, a nice refreshing beverage to go alongside your pit but once you've learned to recognize mature fireweed then it becomes much easier to spot young fireweed.

Young Fireweed

In the spring the young shoots of fireweed emerge from the ground, flaunting those slender lawn shaped leaves and smooth slender stems.

Both of which will often have a bright red tinge to them and as far as edibility is concerned the redder the better.

As those are sweeter in taste all of these above ground parts are edible in raw. You can gaze upon the whole lot but the real prize is beneath the soil. Stick your knife in the ground and pull up the roots and you will find a humongously long horizontal taproot which is full of carbs, sugars and calories.

A top-tier survival food plus much like the red foliage this long hearty taproot who actually tastes quite sweet.

Harvesting Fireweed

Fireweed is one of the most invasive, destructive and stubborn types of weeds. Fireweed can grow anywhere between two to five meters high and is highly resistant to most common herbicides. It can grow in the shade or in the sun, where it prefers a warm climate.

When harvesting fireweed, it is important to act quickly. Harvesting after the plant has flowered and starts to die back may harm or kill the plant. It is best to do your harvesting in the wild when the plant is in full growth. This is the only way to ensure that you have completely harvested all of the fireweed. Do not harvest more than one stem at a time. If you try to harvest more stems at once, the plant may become confused and shoot off too many stems.

When you are ready to remove the stems from the fireweed plant, you should wear latex gloves. This will help you to protect your hands from smoke and sparks as you cut the plant. It is important to cut the plant at a 45 degree angle. Use a sharp knife and make sure you are wearing a mask to prevent inhaling the smoke. Do not try to remove as much foliage as possible as this will result in more leaves for your garden to collect. Harvest the whole plant rather than cutting individual stems and leaving the plant to die back.

Once the fireweed is dead or you have removed all the stem and root, throw the plant in a trash container. Fireweed does not decompose well and will most likely die within a few weeks. It is important to note that you should never re-grow a fireweed plant from a stem or root. After firewood harvesting in wild, you might notice new plants popping up around the area but this is normal and will happen again.

It might be helpful to place a small flagstone or wooden stake in the area you harvested your fireweed from. This will help discourage deer and other wildlife into eating them. Fireweed can make a tough task on your garden by growing very quickly. It can easily overtake a garden in a very short period of time and is very difficult to keep dead. Fireweed harvesting in the wild is a great way to enjoy an abundant garden once again.

2.4 Dandelion

It is a familiar face common in all terrains, a bright yellow sunburst flower and large jagged teeth like leaves.

They are easy to identify and are completely safe to eat. The larger older leaves tend to be quite bitter and so the smaller fresher leaves are typically favored.

Once a popular salad green, all parts of the plant are rich in potassium and iron, more than spinach. A buried nourishing plant to consume but aside from the flowers and leaves the roots of the dandelion are technically edible too, although are usually far too bitter to enjoy.

However, if you were to roast the roots until brown, grind until fine and then brew into hot water.

Then you can make yourself dandelion coffee which is delicious, lacking in caffeine. It is a very pleasant substitute for the real thing.

So, while considering a weed and a nuisance in modern life, here in the wild the dandelion is a high-value natural resource and is a safe choice for a snack. As a bonus the leaves of dandelion are considerably high in iron nutrient, that is very useful in combating fatigue.

Dandelion Harvesting

Dandelion can be found all over the world. The wild dandelion plant usually grows wild on high mountains. However, they can also be found in deciduous woods in the United States. Dandelion can be found on hillsides, along road sides, and even in fields near vegetable crops and livestock. The dandelion is highly adaptable to a variety of soil and conditions, so they are easy to grow.

Wild dandelion can be harvested for their foliage, which is a dark purple, dandelion plant with small flowers. These flowers appear to be about three times as big as the plant. The leaves can be green, blue, brown or even gray in color, and the flowers can have up to 20 stamens or petals. Each dandelion leaf has a number that represents the number of stamens on the flower. Dandelion leaves are commonly used as a vegetable.

It has now spread into many other parts of North America and the world as an ornamental grass. Dandelions typically grow tall and thin, up to six feet tall. As a climbing vine, it can be found on fences, walls, gates and other structures. The flower heads may be useful for creating a decorative fence, providing protection from the elements and nesting insect eggs beneath the flower heads.

Wild dandelion shoots and roots are especially good for gardeners because of the large number of nutrients they contain. Dandelion shoots contain an excellent source of calcium, making them good for growing vegetables. The roots of the dandelion plant can be used for producing root vegetables, such as dandelion root stock and dandelion root. Other dandelion products that can be used as a natural organic gardening aid include the following: dandelion pitchers, dandelion root tea, and dandelion fritter.

Wild dandelion plants also attract beneficial insect predators. These include ladybirds, lacewings, spider mites, ground beetles and even some predatory birds, as well as predatory insects like wasps and aphids. Many types of birds prefer dandelion to other garden plants. They enjoy eating dandelion leaves, flowers and even fruit. These tasty and nutritious plants provide a delicious way to add color and taste to your soil. With little effort, you can transform your lawn or garden to include dandelion as part of your landscape.

2.5 Stinging Nettles

They are notorious for the sharp stinging nettles that cover the plant.

Stinging nettles, providing they are handled correctly can be an incredibly vitamin rich food source for a hungry hiker.

With heart or arrow-head shaped leaves which are heavily serrated all along the edges and droopy hanging flowers, when in bloom the nettles protect themselves from would-be attackers by surrounding themselves insharp hypodermic needles.

They would inject a stinging acid upon touch making it quite bothersome to handle but durable.

If you're wearing gloves then it's easy life but if not, sacrifice a piece of clothing to be used as a nettle grabber and rip yourself up a good handful, favoring the top portions of the plants, as the fresher the leaves the better. Then all of those pesky stinging needles can be quite easily removed by simply holding them in the flames of your campfire.

The heat will completely destroy the needles leaving the nettles, now safe to handle and easy to eat. Nettle leaves are naturally rich in vitamin C, iron, and protein. Effective in combating the malnourishment that accompanies starvation. Since they are so widespread and there's no bitter taste holding you back then you can really stock up on the ions and proteins that will keep your body fit and strong.

But while out on your travels you may also encounter nettles that do not have droopy hanging buds but instead have plump white flowers. These are known as dead-nettles which are unrelated to stinging nettles but regardless are equal in almost every respect with the one exception being that the white flower deadnettles do not have any stinging needles.

They are harmless to handle and thus are typically favored for that's convenience.

2.6 Daisy

Small and inconspicuous, this petite and penny size grassland flower is another read of all to add to the collection.

It's a central yellow disc, thin wiry stems and the white halo of petals are all completely safe to eat. So, for an adventurer wandering through the plains, grassy wooden clearings than a handful of daisies make for a quick on-the-fly burst of energy.

But, why not supersize that meal with the moon daisy, otherwise known as the ox-eye daisy. Bigger and bolder in every respect the old ox-eye is a Daisy on steroids, knee height, and ten times in size.

Its yellow and white frilly flower heads are a substantial source of food typically found in meadows and underneath open-canopy forests. It also features furry stems and serrated succulent almost cactus-looking leaves which is a key feature that separates it from look-alikes such as dog fennel which has thin wiry leaves.

But, pretty though ox-eye maybe, their scent however is one of the worst. Another unique identifier of this plant is that when the flower is crushed or damaged then it will release a pungent and nauseating odor.

A strong deterrent it truly is foul, certainly not anybody's first choice for a v-day bouquet but this is slightly offset by its central yellow disc tasting lightly of pineapples. So, an absolutely delicious taste to compensate for its noxious scent.

Harvesting Daisy

Daisies are very easy to grow and can even be self-supporting when you know how to protect and nurture them properly. This type of plant usually grows up to eight meters high, blooming from two to six stalks, each with between five to eight petals. They normally yellow to purple in color, but may turn pinkish when fully grown. Beautiful daisy orchids are rare, but you can easily locate some near your home.

Wild daisies may be collected from the wild orchid garden or cut down for use in making wreaths and bouquets. You may also purchase ready-to-harvest seed bundles or young plants from a reputable nursery. You can even purchase them online at reputable stores specializing in exotic plants and seeds.

Once the daisy has matured enough to bear fruit, you can harvest them at your leisure. Make sure that the daisies are completely ripe before picking. They should be firm but not bitter. If they are sour or have brown spots, they are too young to produce good fruit. Daisies can be eaten raw or used in jams, salads, or any number of other delicious dishes.

The best time to plant and grow daisies is late spring through summer. The last days of winter won't kill your daisy, but the lack of moisture and warmth will not allow them to produce healthy blooms. When you pick wild daisies, it's important to pick carefully. They tend to get a bit floppy as they grow. You will need to pluck them frequently to keep them from being brittle. If the petals of a daisy fall off, they can be plucked and dried for later use.

In early spring, it is best to hand-pick wild daisies. You can also look for birds' nests and other piles of droppings in the area. The nests and droppings contain a great deal of pollen. When you collect the pollen, take it back to your plant nursery. Many plants breed better when they are supplemented with wild daisies.

2.7 Hawthorn

You've likely heard the red berries should be avoided because they are poisonous and while this may be true in most cases there are of course exceptions.

One of those exceptions being the Hawthorn.

A woody tree that produces bundles of bright red edible berries. When identifying fruit trees, it's usually the leaves that you must scrutinize over as they are likely to be the most unique features.

In the case of the Hawthorn. its leaves are glossy and dark green divided into sections and are deeply lobed meaning that they have protrusions stick out rather than being all rounded.

While the berries themselves are glossy bright blood-red and have a large black crater down in the base of the berry. An absolutely key feature that helps with identification.

Once, you're sure you've got the right stuff, Then these berries can be eaten raw fresh off the tree. However, inside of each berry is a large pipe or stone that will shatter your teeth if you are too hasty squeeze the fruit first, pushing the stone out, and then chow down on the tasty flesh of the fruit.

True to its name the branches of Hawthorn do indeed contain sharp thorns, which is inconvenient but a feature that also helps in identification. Do mind your fingers, but if you haven't already filled yourself up on the fruits of Hawthorn then you can also eat the leaves. Pleasant with a slightly appley taste, they can be eaten raw straight off the tree. While the berries appear later in the year during the summer and autumn the leaves however are available during the spring a time where wild food sources are rather scarce.

Hawthorn Harvesting:

Hawthorn is a beautiful deciduous plant that can be grown both in the wild and in the field. Hawthorn is an evergreen tree, which means that it may die after its flowering, but will begin to grow again the next year. The tree is very tolerant of poor soils and dry air, however, so if you wish to plant it, you must be prepared to provide a rich loamy soil, plenty of sunshine and good drainage.

Hawthorn harvesting in wild has been carried out for centuries. This has made Hawthorn one of the most widely grown ornamental trees for gardens, parks and conservatories across the world. Hawthorn is an evergreen tree that grows up to three meters tall, and flowers in a long-term cycle. It blooms from two to eight flowers in spring, and four to eight flowers in summer. The tree blooms throughout the year, but is particularly active in winter. The leaves drop in the fall and the tree sends down new shoots in the spring.

Hawthorn makes an excellent specimen tree, because it is small enough to easily be placed indoors with minimal pruning. It also has very attractive foliage that is ideal for pruning. In fact, it is one of the easiest trees to grow that does not need any fertilizer. Hawthorn can be harvested in several different ways. One method of harvesting involves cutting the stems so that the branches drop off. It is also possible to hang the berries over a wire cage to kill them. Hawthorn berries can be eaten just as they are. They make a delicious breakfast cereal and are also delicious raw snacks. Hawthorn is often used in tea, either hot or iced. Hawthorn has also been used in bread dough to thicken it. It is considered a beneficial addition to yogurt and other dairy products.

Hawthorn can be gathered from wild bushes around North America. It can also be gathered from gardens. Hawthorn harvesting in the wild is both easy and successful if the grower follows some basic guidelines. The plant is known to produce strong berries, which are easy to juice, and they also do well as a natural diuretic.

Hawthorn berries are highly useful in jams, jellies, ice cream, and juices. You can chew the seeds to release the large amount of sap called cellulose. When you juice the fruit, it will also produce a sweet syrup called caraway in some raspberries and blackberries. Hawthorn is also excellent in making bread.

2.8 Rowan berry

Another tree which bears bright red fruits is the Rowan tree otherwise known as mountain ash.

Likewise as with hawthorn it is the shape of the leaves that you must first scrutinize. Rowan leaves are incredibly divided with each leaf being composed of around 15 individual leaflets which are sharply toothed or serrated all along the edges. Moreover, they resemble ladder rungs and are very reminiscent of burn fronds.

With the berries themselves being orangey red in color with a small brown star-shaped stud right in the base of the berry. However these berries are toxic when they are raw. These must not be eaten straight off the tree as they contain a toxin known as big acid which will make you incredibly sick. However this toxin is completely destroyed by heat.

So, cooking your Rowan berries in a pot of boiling water will render them completely harmless and safe to eat. As a bonus, Rowan's do not contain any large teeth shattering stones so once boiled, you can really just sit back and shove them in, they're good to go.

Cooked Rowan berries are naturally high in vitamin C, so they are a healthy and nutritious burst of sugars and vital energy.

2.9 Garlic Mustard

Edible leaves with a spicy oniony taste, garlic mustard is a highly prized wild food. It is found throughout the woodland, with a preference towards the banks of rivers and ponds.

It is capable of reaching heights of one meter and grows in abundance wherever you may find. It features crinkled heart-shaped leaves with netted serrations, smooth slender stems and clusters of four petaled cross shaped white flowers which seem comparatively small to the rest of the plant.

Overall, it is a simple plant quite easy to overlook but its most significant and unmistakable feature is that when the leaves are crushed, then they will release the strong pungent scent of garlic. It is a foolproof method of identification.

Considered one of the best tasting plants that you can find out here in the wild. Its edible parts include the fresh leaves, the stems the, white flowers and the vertical with seed pods.

All parts of the plants have a strong garlic and onion flavor with the fresh leaves having the strongest taste. A welcome change from the comparatively bland taste of other edibles is tasty leaves appear early in the spring and last throughout the autumn.

So, not only is it delicious but it is also widely available. You should favor the top portions of the planters; they contain all edible components and are much fresher and flavorsome. So delicious, in fact that they were once a staple herb in European cuisine, frequently added to salads for a spicy kick.

Nowadays though the plant has lost its luster and is now considered an invasive weed. As it dominates and over crowds to local flora, eventually colonizing entire ways of land which makes it a menace to the ecosystem. but very convenient to those looking for food.

Due to its abundance, its ease of identification of every part of the plant being edible and its year-round availability, it is arguably one of the best wild foods that you can find while out in the sticks.

Eating as much of it actually helps the environment, rather than harms it. With no guilt you can graze upon a lot for a spicy and filling ancestor approved source of food.

2.10 Red clover

It is famous for its vast carpets of free or for leave shamrocks, a universally recognized symbol of good luck.

The clover boasts a bulbous edible flower which is a surprisingly good source of protein. It is reddish pink in color with each flower being composed of hundreds of small individual tubular florets.

They flower from the late spring, all the way up until the early frost of winter. Location depending, the flower heads will contain 20% protein.

You can expect at least 10 grams of protein per 100 grams, giving it a higher protein content than both spinach and kale combined. Making it a top choice in wild food as a higher protein content always equates to a higher calorie content.

Despite the flower heads being striking and easy to ID, it is theleaves of the plant that really sealed a deal. Trifoliate in groups of free upon each individual leaflet there will be a distinct white, crescent-shaped chevron.

This is an absolutely critical feature as the presence of chevron's indicates that this is an edible species. Both the protein-rich flower heads and the beautiful carpets of leaves are all nutritious and safe to eat.

They are edible in raw form but better boiled to make them easier for your body to digest. You will also find that both parts have a mild sweetness to them. Very similar to the taste of peas which is no surprise being as botanically, the clover does belong to the same family as the common pea and historically due to their pleasant taste calorie content and nutritional value, clovers were once a go to famine food.

It is an available alternative food source in times where not much else available.

With those patches of leaves being absolutely plentiful, the protein-rich flower heads being substantial, and its past history as a famine food, the clover has earned itself the reputation of being a top-tier survival food.

Also clovers can be found in a white pale cream-colored variety which aside from color is equal in every respect.

Red Clover Harvesting in Wild

Red clover, native to North America, is an herb that grows in fields and across the country. It is a perennial herb and the flowers usually appear in the spring. The plant grows as tall as six feet. There are three main types of red clover: Purple Sage, Milkweed, and Red Sage.

There are many benefits to red clover harvesting in the wild. Harvesting this type of clover allows the farmers to get the herb quickly when it is in bloom. Farmers who grow red clover in the wild also get to use the crop they harvest for making pills, teas, and various remedies. They also sell the seeds at market or to gardeners for growing other plants. It takes much less time to harvest these clover plants than it does to grow them indoors in a garden.

The herb has many uses for humans. The plant has been used for coughs, colds, flu, arthritis, stomach aches, flatulence, menstrual pains, diarrhea, urinary problems, worms, indigestion, headache, sore throat, and rheumatism. Many of these conditions can be relieved by taking red clover as a supplement on a regular basis. It can be taken in capsule form or in a tincture (liquid) form. Some of the teas make great hot drinks on a hot sunny day. It can be used in combination with other herbs for treating respiratory and circulatory problems.

Many herbalists recommend red clover for those who suffer from allergies, asthma, migraines, sinusitis, and stress. It is thought to be beneficial for women during their second and third trimester of pregnancy, as well as for women who are breastfeeding. When taken as a dietary supplement, red clover has also been shown to lower cholesterol levels, regulate blood sugar levels, and stimulate the immune system. All these things can help to combat disease and illness, which is why red clover harvesting in the wild is often recommended to those who need extra strength in their immune systems and for the general wellness of their bodies.

There are many different herbs that can be harvested from the wild, but red clover is the most commonly collected herb because of its ease of growth and its many benefits. The red clover plant is quite easy to grow, even in containers, and it will provide a continuous supply of herbs whenever it is needed. The herb is fast growing and can grow up to eight feet high. The large and varied herb family includes over 60 different species, which makes it very easy to maintain. Harvesting the herb is simple and usually not that serious of a task. Those who live in the country, where there is no fencing or other security measures around the herb garden, can enjoy the fresh red clover herb right out of the garden.

It's important to understand that not all red clover is created equal. Some red clover varieties come from fields that aren't in cultivation, such as fields in the middle of a corn field that have been converted to pasture. This means that although they may contain all of the good ingredients for a delicious and nutritious herb, they won't have the health benefits and medicinal properties that would come with cultivation. Others are even harvested from areas that aren't near any crops at all. These herbs tend to contain a higher concentration of important nutrients that will benefit people on a daily basis, but because it isn't being marketed to consumers, it's not going to build up in the soil and get harvested by means of machines and tractors. Knowing which varieties to get, will depend on what you hope to get from the herb.

2.11 Knapweed

From a distance, it's pink firework of a bloom looks a lot like a fissile but upclose it resembles a clover.

In that it's tight and tidy neat looking flower head is actually composed of dozens of individual pink and white tip florets, and it's seemingly a hybrid of two familiar edibles.

The knapweed offers itself as yet another nourishing source of wild food. Unlike its fissile doppel-ganger this plant does not have any sharp needles or spikes. It is smooth and easy to handle. The pink flowers of knapweed are completely safe to eat. Other parts of the plant can be eaten too although they are usually far too tough and woody to be palatable.

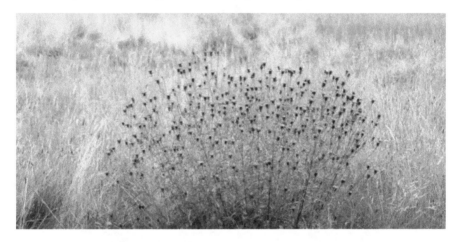

With that, brown pineapple looking but beneath the flower being incredibly tough to chew.

It is like tree bark and this plant has the common nickname of hard heads for that very reason. So, ignore the hard-head and just pluck out the flowers for a sweet tasting and chewy bundle of sugars vitamins and minerals.

Why settle for less when usually not too far away is 'greater knapweed'.

It is identical to knapweed in every respect with the one exception being that additional branched out a ring of florets which gives this great variety of knapweed a much larger and scruffier appearance.

But likewise as with lesser knapweed, the woody scaled bud that bears the flower is far too tough to chew.

So, just pinch away those pinkish purple flowers and then chow down for a quick and easy little troll nibble.

Knapweeds - Harvesting in Wild

Knapweed can be found growing wild along the coastal and central parts. It is a woody vine that grows on fences and walls, climbing up fence posts and fences. The stem of the knapweed plant usually ends up on the ground, wrapped around a shallow root system and drying up. That's why knapweed harvesting in the wild is a little tricky, as the plant has to be carefully uprooted to get at the fruit-bearing leaves.

Harvesting knapweed from the wild can be done without the use of expensive equipment. Since knapweed plants have little aerial roots, you can often get to them by walking along the shoreline, or looking under rocks or cliffs. it would be a good idea to borrow some of your friends' pruning shears, if you have any, and start prying off the knapweed plants with them. If you are caught and try to pull the plants by yourself, be very careful to not damage your own plants by doing so. You don't want to have a huge mess all over the place, do you?

There are a few ways to determine when the knapweed plant is ripe for knapweed harvesting in the wild. One method is to smell the leaves. When the plant starts to change colors, it is time to harvest. Another method is to look for tiny black dots on the underside of the leaves-these are indicators that the knapweed plant has just finished growing and is now ripe for picking. Once the knapweed plant is ripe, you can easily coax it out of its hiding place. First, get a pair of weed spray that has a little bit of water on it, such as the kind that you use for spraying your garden with. Apply the weed spray around the entire leaf body, but leave behind a couple of twigs. When the knapweed starts to sprout, it will push itself out. You can easily grab one of the twigs to push it out.

Some people like to wait for the knapweed to die down before removing the leaves from the stem. Others prefer to get rid of the whole plant, because they find the beautiful flowers pretty enough even without the knapweed stem. Regardless of which you choose, make sure to wash your hands well after you remove the leaves or stalks. Knapweeds are a great wildflower plant to pick up. They grow in large numbers in many regions of the United States. The beautiful yellow flowers are breathtaking and make for a colorful part of any landscape. If you have never done knapweed harvesting in the wild, don't hesitate!

2.12 Burdock

From spring onwards you may find these large clusters of gigantic leaves and this is the burdock which is otherwise known as elephant's ears.

Truly massive, this plant produces leaves that can grow upwards to 3 feet in length. On top the leaves are deeply wrinkled and have a craggy texture.

While underneath they are a much paler shade of green with a light coating of buzzy hairs much like an upscale version of a Primrose leaf, as they both share similar features. The stems too will often have a light coating of fuzzy hairs and will be completely hollow when sliced in half.

They will also be found growing in a tuft, meaning that rather than being one single central main stalk. It is instead composed of multiple individual stalks that all seem to grow out of the same points from within the ground.

Both the elephant ear leaves and the celery like stalks can be eaten completely raw for a substantial bundle of cellulose. There is much more to burdock than just the foliage, as the real prize jewel of this plant is actually the root that's found buried deep beneath the soil.

So, just dig around their big old tough to stems and eventually you will find a very large and long substantial edible taproot.

Being typically 30 centimeters in length and 1 inch in width, the burdock root is the absolute goldmine of wild edible foods.

So, just give it a quick-peel with your knife to remove any of the dirt and then you can eat the whole root raw.

Crunchy watery and tasting mildly like a carrot, it is absolutely packed full of energy and is almost completely equal to potato in calories, carbs and protein content.

So, something really quite special for those on the brink of starvation. Although it is quite a laborious task to dig up that foot long tappero.

It is definitely worthwhile as you will gain significantly more calories by eating it than you will lose through the exertion of digging it. Burdock root is also especially popular in Japanese cuisine where it is known as gobo.

2.13 Elderberry

It is sometimes found as a bush but more often a tree when in woodland environments.

The elder produces enormous and droopy bunches of shiny BB sized black edible berries.

Berries that are considered to be super fruits in that their nutritional value is far superior to other fruit.

It is identified by its large clusters that can host up to 200 berries per bunch. Each berry is a 5 millimeter sized ball that is shiny and deeply purple borderline black when it is fully ripe.

Connecting them are purple or maroon colored stems and on the formless branches are leaves which have heavily rated margins.

The density of the bundle along with how it truly hangs and drops down is how the elder is distinguished from other look-alikes. Such as pokeweed which has no identical berries but grows on aphallic cob and dogwood berries which are far less densely packed have small hairs on the flesh of the berry. Similarly, dull matte black rather than shiny.

Once you're sure you've got the right stuff then these elderberries can be eaten raw fresh off the tree.

Only eat them as long as they are completely ripe. You must avoid eating the unripe and green or red elderberries as they are mildly toxic. Similarly you must also avoid eating the maroon colored stems as those are quite toxic to possessing small quantities of cyanide.

So, real emphasis you must only eat the dark purple ripened fruits only.

Nutritious and full of antioxidants, elderberries contain three times more vitamin C than Tomatoes, twice the protein of apples and double the calories of strawberries. As far as nutritional content goes they put other fruits to shame.

It would of course be wonderful to stumble upon a bunch of fresh strawberries, walnuts and sticks.

Well one should be equally if not evenmore overjoyed to stumble across elderberries as they are the far superior fruit.

Elderberry Harvesting in Wild

The elderberry is a berry that grows on the sides of trees. It has been used for a number of medicinal purposes. Some studies have shown that elderberries can help improve memory, lower blood pressure, decrease cholesterol and regulate diabetes. However, it has not received the same amount of attention as some other natural antioxidants like vitamin C and beta carotene. In Florida, elderberries are harvested from the edges of a bushy tree. This tree, the Smith's Red Oak, is very common in that area. Its berries are sold fresh at farmers markets, but many people grow their own and enjoy eating them canned or dehydrated.

Once the berries are plucked, they go through a couple of processes. First, they're cut into small pieces. Then, they're fried in a pan to cook them. At this point, they have turned into a dark, somewhat sticky berry. You might not think that elderberries can benefit from a campfire. After all, they're meant to be eaten fresh from the tree. But when the berries are fried and placed on a stick, they release their juices. Adding these juices to a cold glass of orange juice makes a delicious drink.

There are a couple of other benefits of elderberry harvesting in the wild. One is that elderberries tend to have a higher vitamin A content than most other berries. This helps prevent free radical damage. Free radical damage is believed to cause wrinkling and other signs of aging. Another advantage of elderberry is that it contains an excellent amount of potassium. Potassium helps your body use calcium, another mineral that can be lost as we age.

So, you can harvest elderberries in the wild. But you should only do so if you've had plenty of time and are comfortable with taking the risk of getting injured. Elderberries are bruised and can result in some nasty cuts. The wild is generally the safest place to try and harvest elderberries. If you're not comfortable with the idea, don't do it. If you are, keep an eye on your plants, and make sure they're in healthy condition.

Once you've picked the fruit from the ground, cut it into small pieces. Thoroughly wash the pieces with water to remove all the foreign matter. Then, take your pickling solution and go through the elderberries' skin, picking out and chopping anything you don't need. Place everything into a large plastic bag and refrigerate until you're ready to use them.

Many elderberry varieties, including those sold at gourmet food stores, are already prepared. You might want to prepare them, instead, but the elderberry flavor will be lost in the paste. You can always just sprinkle the juice over certain desserts or breads to preserve their natural flavor. You'll find elderberries at health food stores and also in many grocery stores. They're sold loose or in bulk. For fresh ones, go to your local berry store. Unfortunately, they're quite expensive. If you're a reasonably good gardener, you could get most of your needs for about one dollar per pound.

2.14 Black berry

The most common of fruits that are easy enough to find when they are in the hedgerow but in the woodland you do not find the blackberry, the black berries find you.

If you've ever had your trousers snagged by thick vines that are late and informed then you have made contact with woodland black berry which in this context are more commonly known as brambles. So, just followed the vine usually through the whole thicket and eventually you will find the otherwise hidden fruits of the black.

Soft, squidgy and composed of multiple drupelets, these fruits are one of the best-known forest foods that can be eaten raw, straight off the bush.

But let that not make us complacent as identification is secured by studying the foliage. With scrambling vines that can grow up to an inch, thick in diameter they are covered in forms and can be either red or green in color.

The leaves which either grow in groups of three or five have very jagged and serrated edges or a dark green on top.

While underneath they are a much paler shade of green and have a long trail of prickles that run down the entire length of the midrib vein.

Providing that you run your knife down the midrib to remove all the prickles then these leaves can be eaten raw - and as a bonus they are evergreen meaning that they will be available all year round as a source of food even throughout the barren midst of winter.

Blackberry Harvesting in Wild

If you love the taste of blackberries and are considering becoming self-sufficient by growing blackberries, you will find that there are a few things you must consider. First, most states prohibit blackberry growing within the state itself. This includes Washington, DC and parts of Virginia. The reason for this is because blackberries have been known to attract deer and other wildlife which can decimate local berries. You must also abide by local ordinances. Some places have restrictions on where blackberry can be harvested, while other places have no restrictions whatsoever.

Fortunately, most places allow blackberries to grow and harvest in the wild. You can find a thriving blackberry market in the Appalachian Mountains region of eastern Kentucky, Maryland, Pennsylvania, and West Virginia. These areas have long been treasured by blackberry enthusiasts. They grow blackberries in fields and on hillsides and they enjoy hiking, picnicking, and dancing to live music played at local outdoor entertainment venues. All kinds of wild blackberries grow in the woods of these areas.

Wild blackberry production can take several forms. There are wet fields where the plants can be harvested by hand. In some cases, the blackberries are simply gathered as they come out of the ground. These berries are still able to be used in cooking and baking recipes but their flavor is often less desirable because they are not as tart.

Still, many people enjoy eating blackberries in their natural state. If you plan to farm blackberries, you will need to know when they are the largest production season for them. In the Appalachian Mountains, blackberry harvesting usually takes place during May and June, with the peak being in July. The blooms tend to be smaller than those found in other climates, so eating blackberries is not a big deal.

For those interested in harvesting blackberries in the wild, there are several methods to use. One of the oldest ways to harvest blackberries is to strap a rope around the plant and drag it through the woods. Sometimes this method results in unexpected results, such as watching a blackberry grow in a strange pattern. To get an expected crop, you can try pruning the plant or rubbing the branches of the blackberry. This can sometimes lead to strange, new growth patterns.

There are many ways to grow blackberries in the wild, which makes them an interesting topic for future books. In the meantime, enjoy catching the seasonal highlights of blackberries in your area.

2.15 Pineapple Weed

Low growing and never more than a foot tall, pineapple weed features a flower head that is corn like in shape.

It is a bulbous yellow and green dome that is seemingly lacking in petals, strange but this is a petalless flower head.

Pineapple weed also features leaves which are thin every wiry spring and true to its name when a part of this plant is crushed or damaged then it will release the sweet delicious scent of pineapples.

A wonderful perk but also a signature characteristic that aids in identification. The bald flowerhead, the stems and the feathery sprawling leaves are all nutritious and safe to eat.

The taste is sweet mildly like a pineapple with a little hint of citrus so eat them raw while in move or perhaps just steep them into a cup of hot water for a delicious and refreshing pineapple scented beverage.

2.16 Rosehip

These bright red and fleshy seed bearing pods are the fruits of the dog rose tree.

A tree which displays small serrated oval-shaped leaves and 5 petaled offwhite or soft pink flowers during the spring through summer.

After pollination those rose flowers will develop into edible red fruits which are known as hips. They are shiny firm and typically oblong in shape with dark brown plugs or tendrils shooting out the bottom. Their unique shape makes them easy to identify and their most unique selling point is that they contain 10 times more vitamin C than oranges.

They contain 420 milligrams of vitamin C per 100 grams as opposed to the comparatively meager 60 milligrams found in oranges. So, any risk of scurvy - no sir, not today. But some preparation is required before you can eat rose hips.

Cut the fruit in half to reveal the innards, inside you will find a cluster of seeds which are covered in horse bristly hairs. These hairy seeds are an irritant and are a choking hazard and so it must be scraped out with a knife until all that remains is clean and smooth tasty flesh. These fruits are now completely harmless and safe to eat so go ahead they're good to go and as a bonus these fruits will contain over three times more calories than apples.

Rosehip Harvesting in the Wild

Rosehip harvesting is based on a method that has been used for many years, although it was not well known among the early settlers. Rosehip plants are tall and very bushy. They grow best when they are planted in thickets or undergrowth close to other plants of different heights. Rosehip flowers have a deep and rich color of orange, pink, yellow, purple and white. Rosehip is the most popular flower grown by gardeners in Florida and along the Eastern seaboard. It is very easy to grow; it does not need much maintenance.

To plant like a flower, the plant needs to have plenty of sunlight and a protected location. Rosehip will bloom twice a year, once in spring and again in autumn. The flowers will rise about four feet high and drop more than three feet to the ground. Each bloom has one feathery petal, with the center being larger than the rest. This creates a stunning show.

Planting locations should be chosen before the flower begins to bloom as there are many weeds and grasses that can destroy rosehip. It can be difficult to get rid of a weed in the winter and in the early spring it may be too late to get rid of the weed. Before the plant starts to flow, if you do find a weed blocking the way, cut it back to allow room for the rosehip to flow freely.

In addition to rosehip blossoms, wildflowers are also planted for the beauty of their blooms and their fragrance. Rosehip will fill your yard up with sweet aromas and look gorgeous with your deck or patio furniture. Some people even grow wildflowers for sale and sell them at local garden shows. There are many types of wildflowers for sale.

There are several things to know before trying rosehip for the first time. Wildflowers are not easy to transplant from one area to another. The best thing is to prepare in advance and start earlier than planned. Rosehip flowers need lots of sun and water, so you have to relocate them in the fall, well in advance of the growing season. Wildflowers need at least six hours of sun each day. If you place them too close to a structure, such as a building, they will not bloom.

If you are looking to plant rose hips for sale, check with local nurseries or grow shops for information on which plants to buy. They can tell you which rosehip trees will produce the most fragrant blooms and which ones will produce the most berries. They can also tell you how much each plant will cost when you go to plant it. There are plenty of varieties to choose from and most nurseries will have pictures of the roses they are selling. All of this information is priceless when you are preparing to harvest wildflowers for sale in wild flower markets or in a garden center.

2.17 Crab Apples

Varying in color from green to red and varying in size from golf ball to cricket ball, wild apples which are known as crab apples are a non-toxic and edible species of apple.

However, they are far too bitter and far too sour to be eaten raw. This is not a bitterness that you can just overcome by manning up. They are so sour and so bitter that they will actually hurt your teeth and temporarily paralyze your facial muscles as the sharp twinge hits you hard.

So harsh in fact that they can often be found intact and on the ground long after they have dropped from the tree suggesting that they are also far too bitter for even animals to consume.

But we are human, capable of cooking and thus the true delicious potential of the crab apple is available to you. So gather your apples ideally those plucked fresh from the tree. Chop them up into tiny pieces and then throw them into a cup of boiling water and keep boiling until all of the water has evaporated away. What you'll be left with is a thick and saucy crab apple puree that is significantly less bitter, a lot more palatable and is incredibly warm and filling. It's good carbs are sugar and good calories as it is all the things needed to help you in fueling your venture.

Harvesting Crabapple in the Wild

Crabapple has a tart and tangy taste that no other citrus fruit can compare to. The fresh juice of Crabapple is very tasty, which makes this fruit an ideal for consumption on its own or even added with some flavors to make it more appetizing. It is one of those fruits that can satisfy almost any kind of taste and preferences.

Before you go crabapple harvesting in the wild, you must be fully prepared and equipped. An important consideration is the presence of sharp objects near the crabapple bushes. You must avoid any kind of sharp object that can injure you. As a beginner, you must start using a bare hands approach and try to snare small ones. This is the most difficult part of Crabapple harvesting in the wild.

2.18 Pine Needles

An evergreen food source available all year.

Around the green and coniferous needles of the pine tree have a fresh and minty taste and can be eaten raw straight from the tree. Although since they tend to grow very high up on the tree you may have to settle for those fallen to ground.

This particular species of pine is scots pine which has three to four inch long needles which always come in pairs of two. However, other species of pine will differ. Pine needles have very little calories and thus they don't have much value as an energy source.

Since they taste so nice and contain tons of vitamin A and C they are more often stepped into hot water to make pine needle tea. It is a refreshing and nutritious minty beverage that will sure as hell break the monotony of drinking the otherwise bland and boring cups of pond water

Conclusion

In this book, we have covered plants that are a very popular food foraging choice. Wild food will add a lot of fiber, potassium, vitamins, and antioxidants to your diet. The main consideration is that once they have been plucked, they are very hard to store, especially in the winter. If you are able to store them, then by all means do so! There are many excellent plant to use as a forage plant when traveling in the wild. The larger white flowers of the plant attract insects and mites and sucking plant juices can help keep insects away.

These are just a few of the edible plants that can be used as forage, along with their potential benefits. Your goal is to find as many of these as possible, in order to have a consistent source of nutrition. There are other edible plants that attract animals, but your goal is to find the ones that are most nutritious to you, and that will not harm you. The more varied your forage becomes, the better off you will be. There are a few other tips that can also be useful, such as making sure your forage contains the correct combination of nutrients you are foraging for. These tips are designed for people that live in rural areas, but it does not matter where you live, if you have a desire to be successful in foraging for survival.

CPSIA information can be obtained
at www.ICGtesting.com
Printed in the USA
BVHW011355090321
601991BV00005BA/170